W9-BYN-397

A Drop of Water

GORDON MORRISON

Houghton Mifflin Company Boston 2006

Walter Lorraine Books

I dedicate this book to the earth for all its wonders, its beauty, its resources, and for all it has given, I am grateful. We owe it our past and our present, and we now owe it our protection, for its future as well as our own.

Walter Lorraine (wn) Books

Copyright © 2006 by Gordon Morrison

All rights reserved. For information about permission
to reproduce selections from this book, write to Permissions,
Houghton Mifflin Company, 215 Park Avenue South,
New York, New York 10003.

www.houghtonmifflinbooks.com

Library of Congress Cataloging-in-Publication Data
Morrison, Gordon.
  A drop of water / Gordon Morrison.
    p. cm.
  ISBN-13: 978-0-618-58557-1
  ISBN-10: 0-618-58557-5
  1. Hydrologic cycle—Juvenile literature. 2. Stream ecology—Juvenile literature. I. Title.
  GB848.M67 2006
  508—dc22
                                                    2006004564

Manufactured in China.
SCP 10 9 8 7 6 5 4 3 2 1

AUTHOR'S NOTE

I have written and illustrated four other children's books. Each of them was about a year in the life of a subject: an eagle, an oak tree, a pond, and a neighborhood. But a year is made up of moments, tens of thousands of moments. And some of the best experiences I have had are when I have taken a moment to consider my surroundings. At those times, whether on a city sidewalk or a mountainside, I'm more aware and appreciative of the things around me, from the seemingly insignificant to the grand.

This is a story about a moment, the time it takes for a drop of water to fall from a child's fingertip. Water is the thread that takes you through the story; from the child, to the clouds, to the mountaintop, then down through forest, woodlands, streams, ponds, and back to the child by the meadow brook. By following this thread we travel through a wondrous landscape and pass plants and animals, including the child, doing what they do: soaring, drinking, eating, blooming, nesting, playing—living, all within the same moment.

The landscape in the story is made up of many places, or habitats. The story is as much about these places as it is about the plants and animals found in them. Each place is different from the next. The deep, dark spruce and fir forest is as different from the sunlit maple and birch woodland as the cold, still upland bog is from the quiet and mysterious lowland swamp. With different plants and different animals growing and living in those places where the conditions are right for them, each place has its own look and feel, smells and sounds.

In another way this book is also about a water cycle, because water is far more than the thread that connects things in a story. Without it there would be no clouds or rain, no forest or bog, no stream, woodland, pond, or meadow, and none of the plants or animals that grow and live in these places would exist. Water and its cycle make life possible on earth.

I hope the words and images in this story give you a sense of what it's like to visit these places. But more than that, I hope you will be inspired to seek out places like these and experience them for yourself. To take in the sights, sounds, scents, and feelings that make each one special. And make it your own.

But you don't have to go to distant places to know the scent of wet earth after a rainfall, the sound of wind through the trees, the surprise of an unexpected view, or the beauty of a flowering shrub; you just have to take a moment, wherever you are, to be aware of your surroundings. And, perhaps, consider all that is going on within the same moment . . .

A child's finger is wet with
water from a meadow brook.
The water moves down the small finger,
and a drop begins to form on the tip.

Above the child,
clouds that brought rain
move apart. The rain is stopping.
The sun is coming out. A passing shower
has cooled a summer day.

Drifting away, the clouds pass
over land, forest and mountain.
Everything is wet from the rain clouds.
A red-tailed hawk soars toward a nearby mountain.

On the mountaintop, rainwater flows out of a forest of spruce and fir trees, with its cool, evergreen-scented air. Down the mountainside it trickles from soil and rock, through cracks and crevices, into a mountain stream.

"Croak-croak." Ravens call out as they fly from the mountainside.

11

The stream tumbles over a cliff,
and the place echoes with the sound of water falling onto rocks below.
A cluster of birch trees stands in the mist of a small waterfall.
Bubbles from the splashing water drift on ripples into a mountain pool.
A thrush perches on a birch branch with hanging catkins.
A red fox drinks from the pool near ferns and mountain laurel.

From the pool the water travels down through the forest. In a flat, open area it slowly spreads and mixes with the cold, still, tea-colored water of an upland bog. A moose pauses in its feeding. Pitcher plants grow in sphagnum moss. A flycatcher flies from its perch on Labrador tea to catch an insect.

The bog is part of
a beaver pond.
A beaver dam, made
of branches and mud,
keeps the water from
rushing away. Flowers of
blue flag bloom around
gnawed tree stumps.
The smooth surface of the water
reflects forest, mountain, and sky.

Water seeping out through the dam rushes downstream.
Over and around rocks it babbles along, through
a changing woodland of sugar maple and yellow birch trees.
A water thrush bobs along the rocks by a viburnum shrub.
A long-tailed weasel eats a small fish caught in one of many pools.

At the woodland edge the stream slows
and spreads into a shallow lowland swamp.
It is a watery place of quiet and mystery,
where red maple trees stand above
a thicket of blueberry shrubs and tussock grass.
Deer drink at its edge. A barred owl roosts
by its cavity nest in a dead tree. And a flock of mallard
ducks are dabbling, surface feeding, in the open water.

From the swamp the shallow water spreads into
an open area of tall grasslike plants, a meadow marsh.
The chatter and chirping of nesting birds fill the air.
A marsh wren scolds a red-winged blackbird. The blackbird has
flown too close to the wren's nest, hidden in the cattail plants.
Bulrush, tall and slender, makes a perfect reflection in the still water.

The marsh is part of a farm pond.
A farmer's dam, made of wood
and earth, keeps the water from
rushing away. The pond is deep and
wide. Yellow pond lilies float on its
surface. Holstein cows drink from it.
Barn swallows also drink from it and
catch flying insects above it. And a meadowlark
sings its sweet song from a fence post.

From the barn doorway the farmer looks out over his pond and meadows. Curling over the dam, water flows from the pond. Passing under a bridge, it meanders, gently twists and turns past timothy grass, painted turtles, leopard frogs, and a child crouching by the meadow brook.

And from
the child's
fingertip
falls . . .
a drop of water.

Page 5. Child: A young human animal, also called a kid. It is curious, smart, and likes to play. Humans are omnivorous, eating both plants and animals. Humans come in many shapes, sizes, and colors.

Water: A colorless, tasteless, transparent liquid. Plants and animals need it to survive. Clouds, rain, mist, snow, ice, sleet, hail, and humidity are all forms of water, a drink without equal.

Page 8. Red-tailed hawk: A large bird of prey often seen in trees at the edge of a meadow. It hunts mallards, meadowlarks, frogs, weasels, and other animals.

Page 10. Raven: A shaggy-throated larger relative of the crow. Living in wilderness areas of mountains, coasts, or plains, they nest on cliffs or in tall evergreen trees. Excellent fliers, ravens often soar like hawks.

Pages 10–11. Spruce and fir forest: A dense growth of fir and spruce trees covering a large mountainous area.

Spruce trees have stiff, sharp needles that curve toward the twig tip. Its cones hang down.

Fir trees have soft needles that curl up and away from the tip. Its cones grow up and crumble on the twig, leaving a spike.

Page 12. White birch tree: Also called paper birch, because its white bark curls back in long papery strips. Native Americans made birch bark canoes from it.

Catkin: A dense cluster of small flowers that hang like a cat's tail.

Hermit thrush: Like the robin, its relative, it usually feeds on the ground. Unlike the robin it often nests on the ground, in forests. The European blackbird, another relative, is one of the "four and twenty blackbirds baked in a pie."

Page 13. Red fox: Found throughout most of North America. Active year round, they live in dens located on slopes. Three to five kits, or young foxes, are born in the spring. The male feeds and protects the female and the kits. By fall the young foxes are on their own.

Interrupted fern: Leaflets curled up against the stem, near the middle of the leaf, give the leaf an "interrupted" look, and its name.

Mountain laurel (spoon wood): Once used to make wooden spoons. Many animals find protection in its dense growth and evergreen foliage, especially in winter.

Page 14. Pitcher plant: An insectivorous plant. The leaves' slippery inner surface and downward pointing hairs force insects to fall or move down into a pool of liquid. There they are slowly liquefied and absorbed.

Sphagnum moss: Also called peat. Millions of small moss plants form a mat on the water around a pond's edge. In time it spreads and grows thick enough to support shrubs and trees.

Alder flycatcher: Inhabits pond edges and bog thickets where its nest is well hidden. Flying from the low perch of a shrub or tree, it catches flying insects.

Page 14. Labrador tea: An evergreen shrub. Birds eat its seeds, and moose and deer eat the buds and twigs. Explorers made tea from its leaves.

Page 15. Moose: The largest member of the deer family. Bull—male, six feet tall at the shoulder and weighing 1,200 pounds. Cow—female, five and a half feet tall at the shoulder and weighing 900 pounds. Calf—stands three feet tall at birth and weighs 35 to 60 pounds.

Page 16. Blue flag: In the year 496, a wild iris inspired the design that, in 1147, was made the symbol of France by King Louis VII. Called fleur-de-Louis, flower of Louis, it later became fleur-de-lis, flower of Lily. But it is not a lily.

Page 17. Beaver: The largest North American rodent cuts down trees, like birch, to eat the bark, buds, and leaves, and to make its dam and lodge. The tail slap on the water warns others of danger.

Page 18. Maple-leaved viburnum: Named for its maple leaf–like shape. Many animals, including the hermit thrush, fox, and deer, find food, shelter, and nesting in the cover of viburnum shrubs.

Water thrush: Although it looks like a thrush and lives where they are found, this bird is a warbler. Its feather patterns and constant body-bobbing help it blend with the dappled light and moving water along woodland streams.

Pages 18–19. Sugar maple: Its sweet sap is used to make maple syrup and candy. For fun, drop one wing of its two-winged fruit and watch it twirl. Split the second wing at the seed end and stick it on your nose.

Yellow birch: Has yellowish bark and fall foliage. Beaver, moose, and deer are just some of the animals that feed on it. Campers know that its bark strips will burn even when wet.

Page 19. Long-tailed weasel: A small carnivore that hunts fish, frogs, birds, and some animals larger than itself. To blend in with the winter snow it grows a special coat, white except for its black-tipped tail.

Page 20. White-tailed deer: Each year male members of the deer family grow antlers. In spring the antlers appear as "buttons" covered in velvety soft skin. The antlers grow through summer. By fall they are full grown and the velvet has been rubbed off. During winter they fall off.

Red maple: Almost everything about this maple is red. Its red flowers grow from red buds. Its red keys, fruit, grow on red stalks, and its foliage turns blazing red in the fall.

Blueberry: Its fruit is an important food for many animals, including humans. Deer and moose also eat the buds, twigs, and foliage.

Pages 20–21. Tussock grass: The tussock "islands" are unstable and tilt when stepped on. But animals rest, hide, or nest on the tufts and eat the plant's seeds.

Mallard ducks: These ducks dabble, or open and close their beaks on the water's surface, letting water into their mouths and straining it out through ridges along their beaks' edge. The tiny plants and animals that remain are swallowed.

Page 21. Barred owl: Its name comes from the barred feather pattern across its chest. On silent wings it hunts, mostly mice, but also frogs, insects, weasels, ducks, blackbirds, and smaller owls.

Page 22. Marsh wren: This bird weaves its ball-shaped nest from cattail leaves lashed to cattail stalks. If other marsh-nesting birds bother the wren, it may destroy or eat their eggs.

Cattail plants: Thousands of tiny seeds from each cattail are spread by the wind. Blackbirds, wrens, ducks, and deer eat the seeds, leaves, and stems; deer and beaver also eat cattail roots.

Page 23. Red-winged blackbird: The male is black with red shoulders. The female's brown colors and patterns help her blend with the nest hidden in the cattails.

Bulrush: Stands of this plant provide food and shelter for many animals, including deer, mallards, wrens, and blackbirds. Humans eat the root stalks raw or cooked, or made into a flour.

Page 24. Holstein cow: Female dairy cattle. Cows produce milk, which humans drink and make into cheese and ice cream. Cattle have horns, not antlers, that remain for life.

Yellow pond lily: A water plant with large oval lily pads, leaves, where frogs may rest. Deer and moose eat the greens, mallards eat the seeds, and beavers store roots for winter food.

Meadowlark: A relative of the blackbird. Its nest is hidden on the ground in a depression, often in a hoof print. It walks fields and meadows, eating insects, seeds, and sprouts.

Page 25. Barn swallow: An insectivore with a small beak and large gaping mouth for scooping flying insects from the air. It often nests on a barn beam.

Page 26. Farmer: An adult human who works a farm where he or she raises plants and animals, such as grass and cattle, to feed people or other animals.

Pages 26–27. Timothy grass: Named after Timothy Hanson, the first farmer to use it for hay, in 1720. It is good for grazing cattle and as hay for winter feed. The meadowlark finds food and shelter in it.

Page 27. Painted turtle: The red and yellow "painted" shell edge gives this animal its name. The one-inch babies, hatching from soft-shelled eggs, are small copies of the seven-inch adults.

Leopard frog: Having spots like a leopard's helps it to hide, especially in meadows, where some adults spend the summer. Meadow frog is its other name.